MW01256946

Diagnosed with Breast Cancer

Life after Shock

Joni Eareckson Tada

New
Growth
Press

www.newgrowthpress.com

New Growth Press, Greensboro, NC 27404
www.newgrowthpress.com
Copyright © 2012 by Joni Eareckson Tada.

All Scripture quotations, unless otherwise indicated, are taken from the *Holy Bible,* New International Version®, NIV®. Copyright © 1973, 1978, 1984 by International Bible Society. Used by permission of Zondervan. All rights reserved.

Scripture quotations marked ESV are taken from the *Holy Bible, English Standard Version®* (ESV®), copyright © 2000, 2001 by Crossway Bibles, a division of Good News Publishers. Used by permission. All rights reserved.

Cover Design: Faceout Books, faceout.com
Typesetting: Lisa Parnell, lparnell.com

ISBN 13: 978-1-938267-78-9
ISBN 13: 978-1-938267-21-5 (eBook)

Library of Congress Cataloging-in-Publication Data
Tada, Joni Eareckson
  Diagnosed with breast cancer : life after shock / Joni Eareckson Tada.
     p. cm.
  Includes bibliographical references and index.
  ISBN 13: 978-1-938267-78-9 (alk. paper)
  1. Tada, Joni Eareckson. 2. Breast—Cancer—Patients—Religious life. 3. Breast—Cancer—Religious aspects—Christianity. I. Title.
  BV4910.33.T33   2012
  248.8'619699449—dc23
                                                    2012024208
Printed in Canada

21 20 19 18 17 16 15 14   4 5 6 7 8

Breast cancer happened to other women, but not me. My attention was always focused on my quadriplegia—forty-five years in a wheelchair saddled me with enough medical challenges without thinking of cancer. *God would never add that to the mix,* I thought. And my most recent mammogram had been nine years earlier.

My attitude changed one morning in the bathroom when I noticed that my right breast was a little misshapen. I called my husband Ken and he confirmed my suspicion. "I feel a lump," he said, "a large one." At first his words bounced off my brain, but then I realized, *So I'm not immune . . . cancer may touch my life after all.* The next day I visited a radiologist. After that, a needle biopsy confirmed what we all suspected. The next thing I knew, I was in the hospital for a mastectomy.

While I was in recovery after the operation, I struggled to come out of my grogginess—especially when I spotted my surgeon on the other side of the room. When he came to my bedside, his words cut through the fog. "Joni, it was a rather large tumor . . . and I had to take a number of lymph nodes that indicated cancer." Those weren't the words I had hoped to hear, but there wasn't time to process such a shocking diagnosis. I had to focus on healing so that I could begin treatment for my Stage III breast cancer—five months of chemotherapy.

Ken was wonderfully supportive, carefully changing my drainage vials every morning and bandaging my wounds every night. Finally, when my chest healed, we visited the oncologist for a rundown on what to expect. He minced no words. I would have to return to the hospital to have a port surgically inserted in my chest. Toxic drugs would weaken my already fragile bones, and blood clots were a risk, as were lung and bladder infections. I would face nausea and hair loss. I'd have to change my diet to ward off fatigue, and on and on. The doctor left the office for a moment, and when he closed the door, I broke down. "I can't do this," I sobbed into Ken's arms. "It's too much, too overwhelming. I can't do it!"

You're in a Good Fight

Cancer is a word that can curdle the blood. The chance of developing invasive breast cancer at some time in a woman's life is around one in eight (twelve percent).[1] For years it was labeled a terminal disease. But the good news is that thanks to improvements in treatment and early detection, millions of women survive breast cancer today.

Whether you're worried about developing breast

cancer, making decisions about treatment, or trying to deal with the ups and downs of chemotherapy, there are things you *can* do to make the most of your battle.

Yes, it is a battle. You are in the battle of your life *(for* your life), but there *is* hope. Millions of women have gone through what you now face, and they have survived. In every community across America, there are breast cancer support groups. October is now known as Breast Cancer Awareness Month. There is plenty of help, information, and hope to go around.

And with Jesus Christ, there is always hope. He even believes your fight against cancer can be a *good* one (1 Timothy 6:12). Even though you may feel as I once did—overwhelmed and fainthearted—you can find courage. It's possible. I discovered wonderful anchors for my soul that buoyed my spirits during the roughest days and beyond. These insights bolstered my soul so much that I just had to pass them along. So I want to offer you real hope with the following facts from God's Word.

1. You're not alone.

The night before I took my first round of chemotherapy, I read Jesus' words in John 21:18: ". . . someone else will dress you and lead you where you do not want to go." The next morning Ken dressed me and took me where I "did not want to go"—a dreaded chemo clinic.

When the nurse drove the needle into my port, I struggled with overwhelming feelings again: *Lord, I'm already a quadriplegic and I deal with pain almost daily. I feel so alone, like you've abandoned me.* Yet, looking at the IV with a steady drip of poison seeping into my veins, the Bible already had an answer for me: "God has said, 'Never will I leave you; never will I forsake you.' So we say with confidence, 'The Lord is my helper; I will not be afraid'" (Hebrews 13:5–6). Jesus, the most God-forsaken man who ever lived, endured our fears and afflictions so that he, in turn, might say to you and me, "I will never forsake you; I will never leave you."

There were times when my faith would vacillate. But I anchored my faith to this response from the psalmist who also fought discouragement: "Whom have I in heaven but you? And earth has nothing I desire besides you. My flesh and my heart may fail, but God is the strength of my heart and my portion forever" (Psalm 73:25–26).

With that first day in chemo, I began the prayerful habit of looking to God's Word for emotional balance, as well as a healthy dose of the *true* reality. I prayed, *Lord, thank you that I'm not alone. You are here, bearing my burdens and caring for my needs. You have not abandoned or forgotten me. Give me your strength for this challenge!*

Friend, you can endure almost anything—even sitting slumped in a big chemo chair—if you know God is sitting next to you. So take heart because the Lord of the Universe is in the battle with you. His love is powerful enough to pull you through. You *can* be more than a conqueror. "For I am convinced that neither death nor life, neither angels nor demons, neither the present nor the future, nor any powers, neither height nor depth, nor anything else in all creation, will be able to separate us from the love of God that is in Christ Jesus our Lord" (Romans 8:38–39).

2. God is sovereign.

The Lord took no pleasure in my diagnosis of breast cancer. For that matter he didn't exactly enjoy my 1967 diving accident, which resulted in a broken neck and total paralysis. Like any father who has compassion on his children, it pained his heart to see me hurt. At the same time, it pleased the Lord to permit my accident. God permits all sorts of things he doesn't delight in.

Lamentations 3:32–33 says, "Though he brings grief, he will show compassion, so great is his unfailing love. *For he does not willingly bring affliction or grief to the children of men"* [italics mine]. Did you read that? Yes, he brings grief, but it doesn't give him joy in doing it. Yes, he permits painful circumstances, but he doesn't get a kick out of seeing us squirm!

Because God's ways are so much higher than ours, he has the capacity to look at your cancer through two lenses—both a narrow lens *and* a wide-angle lens (an analogy I'd like to borrow from Dr. John Piper). When God looks at a disease through a narrow lens, he sees the heartbreak for what it is. It is awful. God feels the sting in his chest when your doctor says, "You have cancer."

However, when God looks at your condition through his wide-angle lens, he sees it in relation to everything leading up to it and flowing from it: How your battle will strengthen your faith, make you more prayerful, inspire and encourage others, give you empathy toward the hurting, draw you, your family, and friends closer together, give you a platform to share your story, and so much more. This is God's wide-angle view of your cancer. He sees a mosaic stretching into eternity, and it is this mosaic with all its parts, both good and bad, that includes his wonderful plan for you.[2]

In the span of a single verse in Lamentations 3, the Bible asserts that the Lord brings grief, yet he does not willingly bring grief. God tried this out on himself. He willed the death of his own Son, but he took no delight in it. God saw how Jesus' death would demonstrate his incomprehensible mercy, as well as bring his people salvation. God often wills what he despises because—and only because—he has a wide-angle view of the world. Meanwhile, we often are limited to a narrow-lens view of our problems. We tend to see the problem only as a painful inconvenience. This is why during chemotherapy I made myself remember that even breast cancer can fit into a beautiful mosaic that one day I will understand. And you will understand too.

3. Keep in step with the Spirit.

Cancer slowed me down. Everything ground to a halt when I got the diagnosis. I cancelled appointments, tabled traveling, and avoided public places (because I couldn't risk catching a cold). No longer in the fast lane, I shifted into low and eased into a slower rhythm for my days. I was impatient with the quieter pace at first, but there was no use feeling frustrated—it was out of my control.

One particular day when I had cabin fever, a friend showed me Galatians 5:25: "Keep in step with the Spirit." The Holy Spirit obviously wanted me to take life in *very* small steps. It happens to anyone who suffers. Life becomes more basic and simple.

On days when I wasn't certain how to fill my time, Ephesians 5:10 told me what to do: "find out what pleases the Lord" and do it. Just do it. So while I stayed home recuperating from various rounds of chemotherapy, I would pray in the morning, "What will please you today, Lord?" I would hear him whisper, *Seeing you eat forty-five grams of protein before lunch.* "And what will please you this afternoon?" *Back away from your computer and enjoy my hummingbirds at your feeder.* "And this evening?" *Give the Food Network a rest and pray.*

Keeping in step with God's Spirit brought Ken and me closer. Many days we would sit in the back-yard and enjoy the breeze or watch the birds in the bird bath. A slower pace brought me and my three sisters closer too. At different times, my sisters flew to California to help Ken with my routines. We spent many evenings snuggled in bed together, watching BBC videos, sharing the same pillow and reminiscing about childhood days back on the farm in Maryland.

Psalm 46:10 commands us to "'Be still, and know that I am God; I will be exalted among the nations, I will be exalted in the earth.'" Cancer may be his way of forcing you to quiet your heart, unburden your mind, and surrender your restless will to him. He wants not only to be exalted among the nations, he's heaven-bent on exalting himself in your life. "This is what the Sovereign LORD, the Holy One of Israel, says: 'In repentance and rest is your salvation, in quietness and trust is your strength, but you would have none of it'" (Isaiah 30:15).

Don't be numbered among those who want nothing to do with rest and quietness. God commands it, and that means that keeping in step with his Spirit is good for your *soul*, as well as good for your battle against cancer.

4. Become an expert.

I know what you're thinking. You assume I mean "become an expert on invasive interductal carcinoma." Spend hours on the Internet comparing the latest findings. Put the American Cancer Society on your "Favorites." Stay up late researching the latest treatments. Join a cancer Facebook page and visit it often. But this is not what I mean by "become an expert."

It is not wrong to know about a disease—knowledge is a good thing. But sometimes the lure to know more and more about breast cancer can dim your enthusiasm for God. What a waste it is to read day and night about carcinomas of the breast and not invest the same time in God. Someone has said, "For every hour you spend researching cancer, spend two hours studying God."

Let this disease drive you deeper into God's Word. "Let us know; let us press on to know the LORD" (Hosea 6:3 ESV). "The people who know their God shall stand firm and take action" (Daniel 11:32 ESV). Finally, our delight should be in the law of the Lord: "and on his law he [the blessed person] meditates day and night. He is like a tree planted by streams of water that yields its fruit in its season, and its leaf does not wither. In all that he does, he prospers" (Psalm 1:2–3 ESV).

Cancer is like a big wall. You can sit at its base and spend hours studying its height and thickness, learning about who built it, how it was designed, which stones were used, and what materials masons might use for future walls. *Or* you can spend hours learning how to scale the wall, to climb to the top to get a better vantage point on God.

Let cancer be like a sheepdog that snaps at your heels, driving you down the road to Calvary where you otherwise might not be inclined to go. Let cancer be like a jackhammer that rattles apart your rocks of resistance. Let it be like a chisel that chips away your pride and self-sufficiency, leaving you more dependent on God.

However you choose to look at it, become an expert in things of the Lord. This cancer—this opportunity—may only pass your way once (Lord willing). As I've heard Dr. John Piper say, "Don't waste your cancer." Of all the things in this world to waste, please do not waste your sufferings. They are a textbook that will teach you not only about yourself, but about your great and compassionate God.

5. Make your days count for eternity.

You used to have a certain rhythm in your days: running errands, picking up your kids from soccer, dropping things off at the cleaners, sipping coffee with friends, and weekly shopping at the market. But now it's all being held hostage by medical appointments and the fatigue that often comes with treatment. This battle is like a big parenthesis in your life, and you find yourself wondering if things will *ever* get back to normal. There are even days when you wonder, *If this is the way it's going to be, is life really worth living?*

Whenever I begin to think my efforts don't count—or even when my quadriplegia and wheelchair feel like too much to handle—I think of a young woman named Kim. Perhaps more than any other person, Kim showed me that my life—*your* life—counts. And it counts more than we can possibly imagine.

I learned about Kim when an elder from her church in Pennsylvania called to ask if I would give her a few words of encouragement. "Kim is a brilliant twenty-six-year-old Christian woman who has always been active in our church," he said, "but last year she contracted a motor-neuron disease and now must stay in bed. She can hardly move and she must be fed with a feeding tube." The elder paused for a moment, then added, "Kim is very depressed and she's wondering if her life is worth living anymore."

I telephoned Kim right away. Her mother tucked the receiver under Kim's ear. Kim's breathing was so faint that I could hardly hear her voice. We discussed many things, including our favorite parts of the Bible, heaven, and prayer. Finally, Kim said with great labor, "Joni, they want to put me on a ventilator to help me breathe, but I don't know if I want one. I'm so tired. Do *you* think I should go on a ventilator?"

called to think of others, no matter how difficult our circumstances.

I suggested to Kim, "The next time your mother tube-feeds you your lunch, why don't you ask to say a blessing on the food before she syringes it into your G-tube?" She thought that was a creative idea. I continued, "Do the divine algebra on that one. It's got to pan out to at least 784 years worth of eternal benefit to you and your mother, as well as glory to God."

What a way for Kim to live out her remaining days. If she were to live only two more weeks with a perspective like this, that figures out to be 14,000 years worth of eternal reward and glory. By the time we finished talking on the phone, my young friend was energized.

It should energize us too. No matter how overwhelmed we feel by cancer and all its attending problems, our lives count. The smile you give others in the waiting room, the notes of encouragement you jot to other patients in the chemo clinic, the doughnuts you bring in for the staff, the phone call of appreciation to your doctor's secretary, the cookies you bake for the women's group that is praying for you—all these things count!

"Therefore we do not lose heart. Though outwardly we are wasting away, yet inwardly we are being renewed day by day. For our light and momentary troubles are achieving for us an eternal glory that far outweighs them all. So we fix our eyes not on what is seen, but on what is unseen. For what is seen is temporary, but what is unseen is eternal" (2 Corinthians 4:16–18). Isn't that wonderful? Your light and momentary troubles are *achieving* for you an eternal glory that far outweighs the inconvenience of any hardship you may face. If you give God a little obedience in a tough situation, he will do his divine calculus; he will multiply out to you one eternal blessing after the next so that your earthly trials will seem like a dim, half-forgotten memory.

Little wonder Psalm 90:12 tells us, "[O Lord], teach us to number our days aright, that we may gain a heart of wisdom." So value your days and make the most of every opportunity to do good because *this* is the kind of wisdom God wants you to apply to your twenty-four-hour slices of time. Life is so short and even James 4:14 asks, "What is your life? You are a mist that appears for a little while and then vanishes." No wonder the Bible describes each day as like a thousand years because that's how priceless they are.

Kim ended up living another month-and-a-half after our phone conversation. But as her mother told me later, those forty-five days—Kim looked at them as

45,000 years—were some of the most meaningful and important weeks she ever lived.

Friend, if Kim made the most of every opportunity to reflect Jesus Christ during those difficult last days of her life, you and I can reflect Jesus throughout our fight against cancer as well. So get a head start on eternity by understanding and investing in the *real* connection between this world and the next. Please know that your prayer, obedience, sacrifice, and Christian encouragement toward others have a direct and positive bearing on your capacity for joy, worship, and service to God in heaven.

Life worth living is not found in a set of circumstances—whether pleasant or painful. Life worth living is found in a person, the Prince of Life, the Resurrection and the Life. Jesus is the Way, the Truth, and the Life. He has the words of life. And Christ the Savior is the One who desires to be Lord of your days, as well as your Wisdom for living. When you look to him each day, each minute and hour, your life will count, and it will count for all eternity. With that, you get an A+ in his divine algebra!

6. Leave the outcome with God.

Now that the most arduous part of treatment is behind me, I wonder, what does the future hold?

As I write, I have a long way to go before I'm declared "cancer free." But this I know for sure: I want to keep the 2 Peter 3:8 perspective on my days. It's what I *must* remember on mornings when I wake up tired and feeling like I can't take any more. You must remember it too. Every day we either nudge our souls closer to heaven or away from it—there's never a middle ground.

And the pain and discomfort connected with this battle has given me a *tiny* glimpse of what my Savior endured to purchase my redemption. The doctors are encouraged about my future and I have every reason to hope that at least at this point, cancer is not my "ticket to heaven." But if my life on earth ends, I know that when I see Jesus, I'll be able to appreciate so much more the scars in his hands. And he will know that my gratitude is sincere and from the heart, for he will recognize me from the fellowship of sharing in his sufferings.

Yes, it's been hard. Jesus hung on the cross so that we wouldn't have to suffer hell, but not so that we wouldn't have to suffer on earth. I'm invigorated because my fight to survive cancer has *meant* something. So if you are still in the throes of chemotherapy or facing a poor prognosis, take courage. Remember that your suffering is giving you something eternally precious in common with Christ.

What if your doctor paints a bleak picture for your future? Well, during my cancer treatment I read a lot of books, but perhaps the best was a short booklet by Dr. John Piper entitled *Don't Waste Your Cancer.* Dr. Piper also battled cancer and he wrote, "Satan's designs and God's designs in our cancer are not the same. God designs to deepen our love for Christ. Cancer does not win if we die. It wins if we fail to cherish Jesus Christ. God's design is to wean us off the breast of the world and feast us on the sufficiency of Christ. It is meant to help us say and feel, '. . . I consider everything a loss compared to the surpassing greatness of knowing Christ Jesus my Lord. . . . For to me, to live is Christ and to die is gain.'"[3]

I repeat, cancer doesn't win if you die. Cancer only wins if you fail to cherish Jesus Christ. Knowing him is ecstasy beyond compare, and it is worth anything to be his friend. So join me in letting this cancer push you deeper into his arms. Cherish him. I have a feeling that you will continue to cherish him, no matter what the outcome!

Endnotes

1. American Cancer Society website, 2011: www
.cancer.org/Cancer/BreastCancer/DetailedGuide/
breast-cancer-key-statistics.

2. This metaphor of God's wide-angle and narrow
lens originated with Dr. John Piper at www.desiring
godministries.org.

3. Philippians 3:8; 1:21.

Simple, Quick, Biblical

Advice on Complicated Counseling Issues
for Pastors, Counselors, and Individuals

MINIBOOK
CATEGORIES

- Personal Change
- Marriage & Parenting
- Medical & Psychiatric Issues
- Women's Issues
- Singles
- Military

USE YOURSELF | GIVE TO A FRIEND | DISPLAY IN YOUR CHURCH OR MINISTRY